AMERICAN CITIES

CHICAGO

Jacqueline S. Cotton

LET'S READ
AV²
BY WEIGL™
ADDED VALUE • AUDIO VISUAL

www.av2books.com

LET'S READ
AV²
BY WEIGL™
ADDED VALUE • AUDIO VISUAL

AV² provides enriched content that supplements and complements this book. Weigl's AV² books strive to create inspired learning and engage young minds in a total learning experience.

Your AV² Media Enhanced books come alive with...

 Audio
Listen to sections of the book read aloud.

 Key Words
Study vocabulary, and complete a matching word activity.

 Video
Watch informative video clips.

 Quizzes
Test your knowledge.

 Embedded Weblinks
Gain additional information for research.

 Slide Show
View images and captions, and prepare a presentation.

 Try This!
Complete activities and hands-on experiments.

... and much, much more!

Go to **www.av2books.com**, and enter this book's unique code.

BOOK CODE

AVV45549

AV² by Weigl brings you media enhanced books that support active learning.

Published by AV² by Weigl
350 5th Avenue, 59th Floor New York, NY 10118
Website: www.av2books.com

Library of Congress Cataloging-in-Publication Data

Names: Cotton, Jacqueline S., author.
Title: Chicago / Jacqueline S. Cotton.
Description: New York, NY : AV2 by Weigl, 2018. | Series: American cities
Identifiers: LCCN 2017049476 (print) | LCCN 2017049816 (ebook) | ISBN
  9781489672964 (Multi User ebook) | ISBN 9781489672957 (hardcover : alk.
  paper) | ISBN 9781489677662 (softcover : alk. paper)
Subjects: LCSH: Chicago (Ill.)--Juvenile literature. | Chicago
  (Ill.)--Guidebooks--Juvenile literature.
Classification: LCC F548.33 (ebook) | LCC F548.33 .C68 2018 (print) | DDC
  977.3/11--dc23
LC record available at https://lccn.loc.gov/2017049476

Printed in the United States of America in Brainerd, Minnesota
1 2 3 4 5 6 7 8 9 0 22 21 20 19 18

032018
150318

Project Coordinator: Heather Kissock   Designer: Ana María Vidal

Weigl acknowledges Getty Images, Alamy, Shutterstock, and iStock as the primary image suppliers for this title.

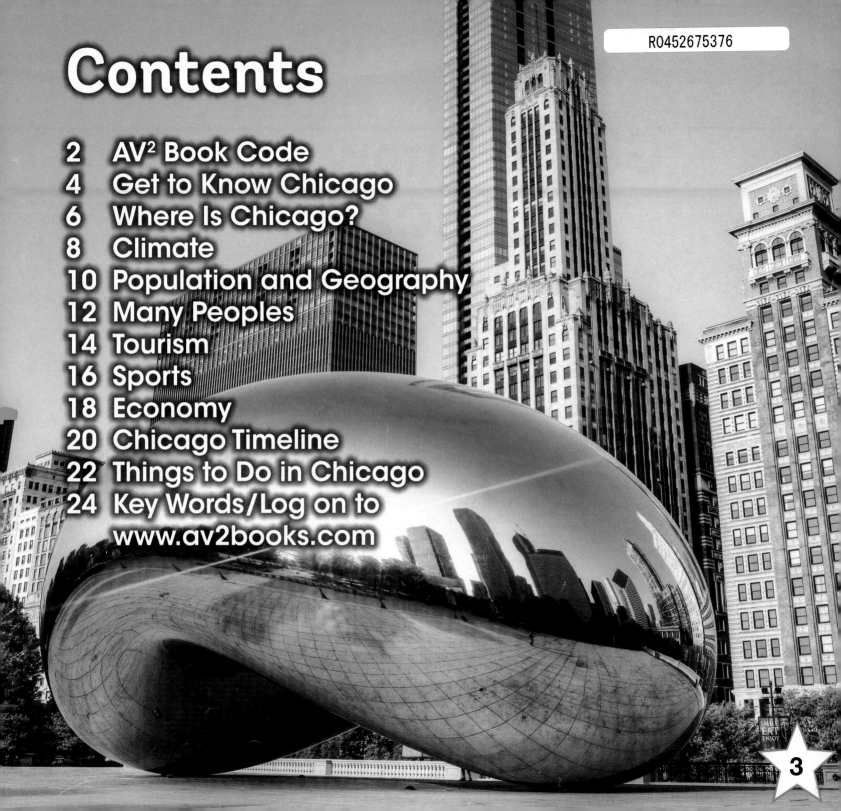

Contents

Get to Know
Chicago

Chicago is the largest city in the state of Illinois. It is well known for its skyscrapers. Willis Tower is one of the tallest buildings in the world.

Map of Illinois

Anderson Japanese Gardens, Rockford

Lake Michigan

CHICAGO

Starved Rock State Park

ILLINOIS

IOWA

INDIANA

● **SPRINGFIELD**

Cahokia Mounds State Historic Site

Shawnee National Forest

MISSOURI

KENTUCKY

United States Map

Illinois

Alaska Hawai'i

MAP LEGEND

☆ Chicago
● Capital City
■ Illinois

▪ United States
□ Water

SCALE 0 ——— 35 Miles

N

Where Is Chicago?

Chicago is in the northeast part of Illinois. It is 202 miles north of Illinois's capital city, Springfield. You can get to Springfield from Chicago by traveling southwest on the I-55 highway.

There are many other places to visit in Illinois. You can use a road map to plan a trip. Which roads could you take from Chicago to get to these places? How long might it take you to get to each place?

TRAVELING ILLINOIS
Chicago to Rockford 94 miles
Chicago to Starved Rock State Park 93 miles
Chicago to Cahokia Mounds State Historic Site 289 miles
Chicago to Shawnee National Forest 337 miles

Climate

Summer in Chicago is hot and humid. Thunderstorms are common. Besides thunder, these storms bring lightning, rain, and sometimes hail.

In the winter, gusts of cold wind blow. The wind makes the air feel colder than it is. Major snow storms pass through the city at times. They cover the city in a blanket of snow.

Chicago is sometimes called **"The Windy City."**

Population and Geography

Almost 3 million people live in Chicago. This makes Chicago the third largest city in the United States. More than half of all the people in Illinois live in or around the city.

Chicago sits on the shore of Lake Michigan, one of the five Great Lakes. The Chicago River flows through the city's downtown. This river is dyed green on St. Patrick's Day.

Many Peoples

Aboriginal Peoples were the first people to live in the Chicago area. In the 1780s, Jean-Baptist-Point du Sable, a trader, started a settlement in Chicago. The U.S. Army built a fort there a few years later.

Soon, people from all around the world started moving to Chicago. Today, people from many different places live in the city.

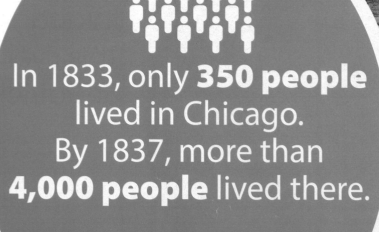

In 1833, only **350 people** lived in Chicago. By 1837, more than **4,000 people** lived there.

Tourism

Visitors to Chicago often stroll along the city's Riverwalk. It runs through downtown along the Chicago River. From the Riverwalk, people can view the city's many skyscrapers.

Every summer, Chicago holds a festival called Taste of Chicago. It lets local restaurants set up booths outdoors and serve samples of their foods.

In 2017, more than **1.5 million people** came to try the foods at **Taste of Chicago**.

Sports

Chicago is home to six major sports teams. The White Sox and the Cubs play baseball. The Cubs' home is Wrigley Field. It is one of the oldest ballparks in the United States.

The Bulls are the city's main basketball team. The Bears play football, and the Blackhawks play hockey. The city's main soccer team is the Fire.

Chicago Timeline

12,000 years ago
Aboriginal Peoples live in the Chicago area.

1837
Chicago becomes a city.

1803
U.S. soldiers build Fort Dearborn in Chicago.

1871
The Great Chicago Fire destroys more than 17,000 buildings.

Economy

Tourism is a big business in Chicago. Every year, more than 50 million people visit the city. They stay in hotels, eat at restaurants, and tour attractions.

Chicago's O'Hare International Airport is one of the busiest airports in the world. People and goods are flown to and from the city.

Almost **80 million** people passed through O'Hare International Airport in **2017**.

1885
The Home Insurance Building, the first skyscraper in the world, is built in Chicago.

2016
The Chicago Cubs win the World Series for the first time in 108 years.

1900
The Chicago River is reversed to flow backwards.

2017
Chicago's train system, called the "L", turns 125 years old.

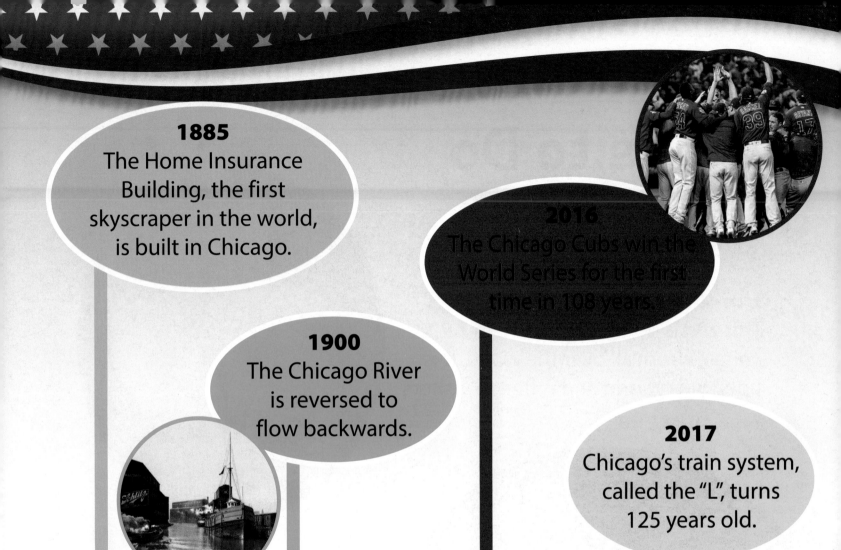

Things to Do in Chicago

Lincoln Park Zoo

This zoo is home to more than 1,200 animals from all over the world. It is open year round and is free to visitors.

Navy Pier

Navy Pier is a popular tourist spot. It has a Ferris wheel that is nearly 200 feet tall and a children's museum.

Willis Tower Skydeck

The Skydeck is found on the 103rd floor of Willis Tower. From here, people can look over four U.S. states.

Field Museum

This natural history museum has the world's largest Tyrannosaurus rex skeleton. It is named Sue.

Millennium Park

People come to Millennium Park to see concerts and to view its interesting art displays.

KEY WORDS

Research has shown that as much as 65 percent of all written material published in English is made up of 300 words. These 300 words cannot be taught using pictures or learned by sounding them out. They must be recognized by sight. This book contains 99 common sight words to help young readers improve their reading fluency and comprehension. This book also teaches young readers several important content words, such as proper nouns. These words are paired with pictures to aid in learning and improve understanding.

Page	Sight Words First Appearance	Page	Content Words First Appearance
4	get, know, to	4	Chicago
5	city, for, in, is, it, its, of, one, state, the, well, world	5	buildings, Illinois, skyscrapers, Willis Tower
7	a, are, by, can, could, each, from, how, long, many, might, miles, on, other, part, places, take, there, these, use, where, which, you	7	highway, map, roads, Springfield, trip
		8	climate, hail, lightning, rain, snow, summer, thunder, thunderstorms, wind, winter
8	air, and, at, makes, sometimes, than, they, through, times	11	downtown, geography, Great Lakes, green, Lake Michigan, population, shore, St. Patrick's Day, United States
11	all, almost, around, live, more, or, people, river, this		
12	different, few, first, later, only, soon, started, were, years	12	Aboriginal Peoples, area, fort, Jean-Baptist-Point du Sable, settlement, trader, U.S. Army
15	along, came, every, foods, lets, often, runs, set, their, try, up	15	booths, festival, restaurants, Riverwalk, samples, Taste of Chicago, tourism, visitors
16	home, play	16	ballparks, baseball, Bears, Blackhawks, Bulls, Cubs, Fire, football, hockey, sports, teams, White Sox, Wrigley Field
19	big, eat, goods	19	attractions, business, economy, hotels, O'Hare International Airport
21	old, turns	20	Fort Dearborn, soldiers, timeline
22	animals, children's, do, feet, has, open, over, that, things	21	Home Insurance Building, system, World Series
23	come, found, four, here, look, named, see	22	Ferris wheel, Lincoln Park Zoo, museum, Navy Pier
		23	concerts, displays, Field Museum, floor, Millennium Park, skeleton, Willis Tower Skydeck